STUDENT HANDBOOK

Your sneaking suspicions?

by Simon Smart

to be used with

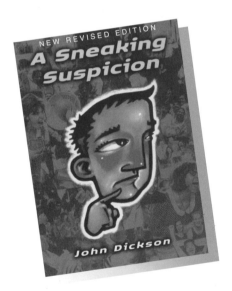

and Your sneaking suspicions? Teacher's Manual

(available from CEP)

Chapter 1

THE SEX FACTOR

To be human means ...

_____

_____

On page 13, the author says that the promoters of sexual freedom in reality are demoters. What does he mean by this?

_____

_____

What does the author mean by 'sex is meant to be an expression of a relationship'? (page 15)

_____

_____

© Chris Morgan www.cxmedia.com

Permissive society

Wake, for the dawn has put
the stars to flight,
And in my bed a stranger:
so once more,
What seemed a good idea last night
Appears, this morning,
sober, rather poor.

Connie Bensley[1]

Relationships

Good Stuff	Bad Stuff

 How relevant are these things when discussing sexual relationships?

_____

On page 16, the author talks about the danger of heading toward a 'hollow, confusing and even harmful view of sex – one that threatens to ruin our relationships'.

Agree? /Disagree? /Explain

 Porsche or Datsun
List ways of living that reflect these two attitudes to sex.

The 'Porsche' approach

_____

_____

The 'Datsun' approach

_____

_____

_____

'They haven't invented a condom that will protect your self-respect or your heart from being broken'

(Jason Stevens, _Worth the Wait_)[2]

Do you agree that placing the highest value on sex would mean preserving it for a life-long commitment? What do you find positive about such an approach? What do you find negative? What do you find interesting?

_____

_____

_____

_____

What is meant by the sexual experience being 'a whole person experience'?

_____

_____

_____

'... while extreme violence and sexual assault is foundational in the animal kingdom, it cannot be tolerated amongst humans. But why? Doesn't it assume that there is some type of qualitative moral difference between animals and humans?'

(Michael Spielman)[5]

Nothing but mammals?

'You and me baby ain't nothin' but mammals So let's do it like they do on the Discovery Channel'

(The Bloodhound Gang)[3]

'The Bible tells us who we are ... We do not need to be confused, as is much of modern mankind, about people's distinction from both animal life and ... complicated machines ... Suddenly people have unique value.'

(Francis Schaeffer)[4]

What do these two views mean for our relationships?

The Bloodhound Gang	Francis Schaeffer

Sex is?

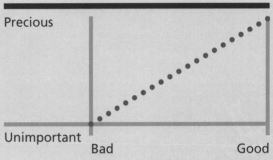

Precious

Unimportant

Bad   Good

- Show on this graph the point where the author of *A sneaking suspicion* says the Bible places sex.
- Where do you think society as a whole would put sex on this graph?
- Where on the graph is your own attitude to sex?

How do you respond to the idea that God invented sex to be enjoyable, intimate, and exciting, and that he provides guidelines and rules to enhance enjoyment and guard against hurting others and being hurt ourselves?

_____

_____

_____

_____

The point of no return

What does the story of Jesus and the woman teach us if we have made mistakes in the area of sex?

_____

_____

_____

_____

Chapter 2

THE BEAUTY MYTH

 My role models

_____

_____

_____

What they are famous for

_____

_____

_____

'It's possible to have such an unhealthy emphasis on our outside appearance that the inside wastes away.' (page 23)

Describe a healthy attitude to our outside appearance.

_____

_____

_____

'That's just something ugly people say'

(Jim Carey in Liar Liar in response to his son's question 'Isn't real beauty on the inside?')[1]

What things tell us that our society is obsessed with image and having the right 'look'?

_____

_____

_____

How do you react to the author's opinion about the danger of an overemphasis on appearance?

_____

_____

_____

Character v 'the look'

Character	Image and 'the look'

'The look that kills

It was reported in *Who Magazine* that in June 2004 just after her high school graduation, Mary Kate Olsen was committed to a treatment centre. Increasingly thin and clearly unhealthy, Mary Kate appears to share a common problem for young people – an eating disorder. 'They finally reached the point where they had to act. They didn't want to find her dead on the floor from not eating.'

(Who magazine)[2]

Costs of the body beautiful
(pages 24–28)

```
My life
Thinking big,
not small
```

THE BIGGEST PICTURE *of all*

God's picture of life, us, and his kingdom

 Write down the 'big picture' messages these Bible passages have for us.

Psalm 139:13–16

Matthew 6:19–24

Proverbs 31:30

What Tiffany discovered

(Read pages 21–22 and 28–29).
What things did Tiffany feel she had learnt through her experiences?

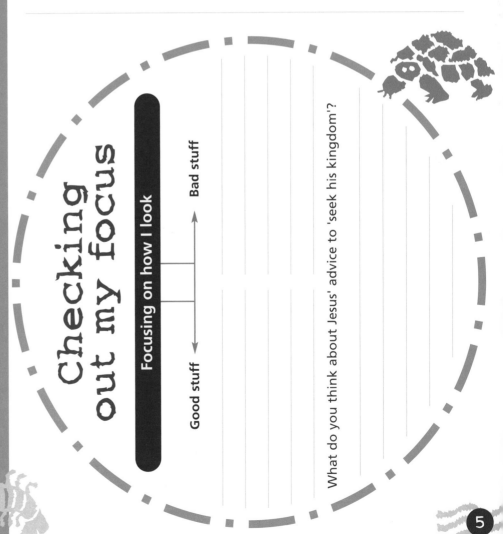

Checking out my focus

Focusing on how I look

Bad stuff

Good stuff

What do you think about Jesus' advice to 'seek his kingdom'?

Chapter 3

RATED "R"

Speech bubble 1: ARRGHH! DON'T play with the PAINT... and who are those men?

Speech bubble 2: I am your son's solicitor. I've been instructed to inform you that this isn't his fault but he'll consider a plea bargain

© Chris Morgan www.cxmedia.com

Whatever happened to right and wrong?

'People don't care much about right and wrong' (page 32)

Do you care? (Read pages 31–33.)

In the past week what has happened in the wider world (or your world) that has been definitely wrong?

_____

_____

Where do your ideas of right and wrong come from?

_____

_____

G U I L T

Read (or listen to) the four scenarios that describe a situation that involves a guilty person. Tick the box that gives the best advice to the person experiencing guilt.

☐ 'Forgive yourself and move onto the next exciting life lesson.'

☐ 'Nothing is as bad as it seems.'

☐ 'Friends will forgive and they will forget.'

☐ 'Ask yourself if this is a situation you will think about in years to come. The answer? probably not, so forget about it!'[1]

☐ 'This is serious. This will involve big consequences. There is a need for a solution.'

What is your solution for dealing with guilt?

_____

_____

What positive function can guilt play in situations like those you have just heard?

_____

My life as a MOVIE

_____
_____
_____
_____
_____
_____
_____
_____
_____
_____
_____
_____
_____
_____
_____

RULES

'The more I considered Christianity, the more I found that while it had established a rule and order, the chief aim of that order was to give room for good things to run wild!'

G.K Chesterton
Orthodoxy[2]

? 'God's rules are a lot like the rules of your favourite sport – they are not there to ruin the game, but to make the most of the game.'

Do you agree or disagree?

Read pages 33 to 34

 'God's rules are good' (page 34)

 If people followed God's rules the world would be like this.

When people ignore God's rules the world is like this.

Fill the box with words and images

? Is guilt ever appropriate? Could guilt ever be good for you?

What do you think about the claim that Jesus came to offer forgiveness? What questions do you have about this concept?

Why do you think some people accept this offer and others choose to ignore it?

Chapter 4

THE SURPRISE OF MY LIFE

Hey... that's a Christian driving a cool car!

I didn't know Christians could drive...

© Chris Morgan www.cxmedia.com

Perceptions: Christians

What was the author's 'most startling discovery'?

What did the author originally think about God?

What did he discover about God?

What do you think is meant by saying that God's love was a 'gutsy' kind of love? (page 40)

What I think about God:

'[when a person's mind] begins to concern itself with God, it is baffled. It gropes in the dark. It flounders out of its depth. It is lost . . . but God has spoken. He has taken the initiative to reveal himself.'

(John Stott *Basic Christianity*)[1]

What changes took place in the author's life once his friendship with God took off?

I tell you for certain that everyone who hears my message and has faith in the one who sent me has eternal life and will never be condemned. They have already gone from death to life.
John 5:24 (CEV)

What would it take to convince you that Christianity has something to offer?

Sneaking Suspicion Journal Entries

Part One - some sneaking suspicions

Part Two - some nagging doubts

Part Three - the guts of it all

Chapter 5

SCIENCE VS GOD

Extensive scientific testing has led us to the conclusion that there is, in fact, no "Baker"

© Chris Morgan www.cxmedia.com

Is God still relevant?
Round one:
the deposed queen

Getting rid of God

? How did science and philosophy combine to dismiss faith in God?

Galileo incident

_____

Darwin

_____

Nietzsche

_____

Round two: God back in the ring

The author has tried to show that belief in God is neither unscientific nor unintelligent. Do you agree with him?

_____
_____
_____
_____
_____
_____

Human life – how important?

People are special and human life is sacred, whether or not we admit it . . . Every person is worth fighting for, regardless of whether he is young or old, sick or well, child or adult, born or unborn, or brown, red, yellow, black or white.

(Francis Schaeffer)[1]

 What do you think of these two opposing ideas?

_____
_____
_____
_____
_____

The extinction of many types of people is just as desirable as any form of reproduction . . . the tendency must be towards the rendering extinct of the wretched, the deformed, the degenerate . . .

(Friedrich Nietzsche)[2]

Round Three: the bout is called off

'Science is a good tool. If you want to work out how the universe began or cure diseases, if you want to work out whether drinking water is better clean or dirty, science is good for that. A hammer is a good tool for a carpenter. Your chef wouldn't use it a lot, so science is not the right tool for analysing life. It took me . . . a long time to realise this which is probably why most of my relationships weren't good in the early days.'

(Dr Karl Kruszelnicki)[3]

'If only God would give me some clear sign! Like making a large deposit in my name at a Swiss bank!'

(Woody Allen, *Without Feathers*)[4]

What do you think?

In what areas of life do you think science is useful? In what areas of life do you think science has nothing to contribute?

Science

_____

_____

_____

Non-science

_____

_____

_____

'Knowing why we are here is not only fascinating – it's crucial for our fulfilment and happiness.' (page 51) Do you agree or disagree? Why?

_____

_____

_____

'I shall always be convinced that a watch proves a watchmaker and a universe proves a God.'

(Voltaire – French thinker)[5]

'We live in the most scientifically advanced age and yet people are still longing for answers.' (page 50)

How much do you think longing for answers occupies the thoughts of the average Australian?

_____

The designer's purpose

What is meant by 'the more we neglect the "spiritual" dimension to the big questions of life the more … we're going to be let down, frustrated and in some cases despairing'? (page 53)

What do you think are the big questions of life?

'We need a place we can draw the fabric of our values from . . . that gives us a purpose, a hope, the ability to go on.' (Peter Garrett, page 53)

From where do you get your purpose and hope?

The Christian faith claims the great designer has entered our world in the person of Jesus. What do you think Jesus has to teach us about the purpose of our lives?

Chapter 6

BIBLE MYTHS

So, why don't you want this map of the world?

It's over a year old! It's hardly going to be relevant today

© Chris Morgan www.cxmedia.com

The Bible is:

What do you think about the Bible? Tick one or more of these statements to indicate your view of the Bible.

☐ History ☐ Truth ☐ Story ☐ Fact ☐ Lie

☐ Irrelevant ☐ Fantasy ☐ God's word to us

The author looks at four myths about the Bible. Identify the four myths about the Bible. Summarise the answer presented by the author. Explain whether you find the answer convincing. Write any other related questions you have.

Explain your opinion:
My view of the Bible

Myth 1

Answer

Convincing?

Other questions?

Myth 3

Answer

Convincing?

Other questions?

Myth 2

Answer

Convincing?

Other questions?

Myth 4

Answer

Convincing?

Other questions?

What is the author's advice at the end of this chapter?

Quick quiz

What is the first book of the Old Testament?

What is the last book of the Old Testament?

What is the first book of the New Testament?

What is the last book of the New Testament?

How many books of the Bible begin with the letter M?

2 Timothy 3:16
Every part of Scripture is God-breathed and useful one way or another — showing us truth, exposing our rebellion, correcting our mistakes, training us to live God's way.[1]

Chapter 7

THE RIDDLE OF SUFFERING

I'm not sure sir, it looks like bird poo...

WHY?!? WHY??? Why does God allow this to happen???

© Chris Morgan www.cxmedia.com

Do you think God cares about our suffering? Explain your opinion.

Does suffering disprove God?

? Do you agree that if there is no God, 'everything that happens – good or bad – must be thought of as the result of the random, mindless, wastage of evolution'? (page 65) Why? Why not?

'She was not well, and I just look at that video and see how beautiful she is - that lovely smile and the kind of hope in her eyes. It just seemed very unfair. Much more unfair than Brett's death. 'Cause she seemed like the innocent that was being punished somehow by a God I don't believe in.'

Wendy Whitely – speaking about the death of her daughter Arkie[1]

What do you think of being angry at 'a God I don't believe in'?

RESPONDING TO SUFFERING

After listening to the stories of how these two men suffered, describe how each one responded to God as a result their suffering.

Prisoner of Nazis

Gerald Sittser

What do these accounts tell you about reactions to suffering?

Does God hate us?

What did Jesus say about the idea that our suffering is pay-back for wrongs we have done?

_____

_____

_____

OUR FREEDOM TO CHOOSE

Explain on the following diagram, the link between humanity's ability to make its own decisions and the chaos and suffering that results.

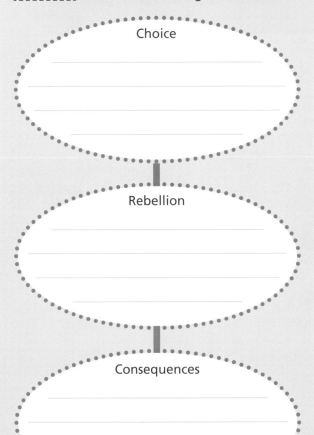

Choice

Rebellion

Consequences

What do you think about the idea that _suffering_ is 'the price God pays in allowing us to accept or reject his friendship'? (page 68)

_____

_____

_____

_____

Things will get better

What comfort and hope does the Bible offer for people experiencing suffering?

DESIGNING GOD

If you were designing God, What would he (or she) be like?

How is Jesus different from your idea of what God should be like?

My design

Jesus

'However, the God spoken of in the Bible does feel our pain. He can fully sympathise because he has greatly suffered.' (page 71)

What difference does it make to know that God has greatly suffered?

_____

'Countless acts by millions of self-centred, instead of God-centred, individuals may reasonably be thought to be destroying the world.'
G.K. Chesterton[2]

Chapter 8

GOD'S ELEPHANT

Over here! It's light out here!

Yeah right! Hey everyone! It's "light" over there!!

Ha Ha Ha

Yeah? Well it's "light" over here as well!

And here! Ow! That's my foot!

Sorry

© Chris Morgan www.cxmedia.com

Just as a particular disease in the world is treated by various medical methods, so there are many religions to bring happiness to human beings and others.'

(The Dalai Lama)[1]

Option 1: Avoid the issue

Why might someone want to avoid the issue of there being many religions?

_____

_____

Is this a good idea?

_____

_____

_____

My option

What do you think about the fact that there are many religions?

_____

_____

Option 2: Accept every possibility

Why do many people accept this option?

_____

_____

What are the weaknesses in this way of thinking?

_____

_____

_____

Option 3: Reject every possibility

According to the Britannica book of the year for 2004, there are 784,269,000 people in the world who regard themselves as non-religious![2]

Why might someone decide to reject all religions as false?

_____

_____

_____

Is this a good idea?

_____

_____

_____

The photograph

Jack Dillon is a computer systems analyst. He has lots of interests outside work.

What can we learn about Jack from the photographs?

LOOKING AT GOD'S PHOTOGRAPH

Jesus

☐ Mad ☐ Fraud ☐ God

What do you think of Jesus?
Tick one of the boxes and explain the reason for your choice.

Are there other possibilities when it comes to Jesus?

Look up the following verses in the Bible. If Jesus is God's photo, what do these passages tell us about what God is like?

Luke 7:11-17

Luke 8:40-48

Matthew 21:12-13

Chapter 9

TOO GOOD FOR GOD

Why God should be friends with me

Rate yourself – Mark out of ten ...

- Patience
- Kindness
- Forgiveness
- Generosity
- Gentleness
- Humility
- Faithfulness to God
- Holiness
- Self-control
- Peacefulness

Dear diary,

Today I left the temple feeling . . .

Pharisee

Dear diary,

Today I left the temple feeling . . .

Tax collector

Approved by God?

The Pharisee

Approved

☐ Yes   ☐ No

Why?

The tax collector

Approved

☐ Yes   ☐ No

Why?

GOD'S STANDARDS VS MY STANDARDS

What problem is created because God's standards are much different from ours?

Draw a diagram to represent the gap between God's standards and our standards.

 Why does the author say that 'being good' is not enough?

Hi... Um... I brought some food... It's only left overs...

You didn't read the invitation either... Put the pizza in the bin and come on in!

© Chris Morgan www.cxmedia.com

Becoming God's friend

In the space below, explain how the author of *A Sneaking Suspicion* says we can become God's friends.

Romans 5:1–2 (NIV)
Therefore, since we have been justified through faith, we have peace with God through our Lord Jesus Christ, through whom we have gained access by faith into this grace in which we now stand. And we rejoice in the hope of the glory of God.

According to this verse, how do we have peace with God?

Chapter 10

THE DEATH FACTOR

So... what are you guys going to do after you die?

I'm going to reincarnate as a pig, get really fat and sleep in mud

I'm tossing up between coming back as a zombie or just going straight to heaven

© Chris Morgan www.cxmedia.com

Death and dying

Read the quotes below and give them a ranking from 0–5.
5 means 'I strongly relate', and 0 means 'I don't relate to this at all'.

☐ I am afraid of death. I try not to think about it, but it is there at the back of my mind and it freaks me out.

☐ I've been to the other side and let me tell you there's nothing there. (Kerry Packer: revived after his heart had stopped beating for seven minutes)[1]

☐ Everyone dies alone!

☐ When we die we go to another, better place.

☐ Life after death is just wishful thinking.

☐ Is death the last sleep? No – it is the last and final awakening.
(Sir Walter Scott)[2]

☐ If man hasn't discovered something that he will die for, he isn't fit to live.
(Dr. Martin Luther King Jr.)[3]

☐ To die will be an awfully big adventure.
(Sir James Barrie, Peter Pan)[4]

I don't want to achieve immortality through my work. I want to achieve it through not dying.
(Woody Allen)[5]

If I think more about death than some other people, it is probably because I love life more than they do.
(Angelina Jolie)[6]

What is a person?

FAT enough for seven bars of soap
IRON enough for one medium sized nail
SUGAR enough for seven cups of tea
LIME enough to whitewash one chicken coop
PHOSPHORUS enough to tip 2200 matches
MAGNESIUM enough for one dose of salts
POTASH enough to explode one toy crane
SULPHUR enough to rid one dog of fleas

(Professor C.E.M Joad)[7]

Psalm 139:1-4, 13-14 (NIV)

1 O LORD , you have searched me and you know me.
2 You know when I sit and when I rise; you perceive my thoughts from afar.
3 You discern my going out and my lying down; you are familiar with all my ways.
4 Before a word is on my tongue you know it completely, O LORD.
13 For you created my inmost being; you knit me together in my mother's womb.
14 I praise you because I am fearfully and wonderfully made; your works are wonderful.

What are the differences between the Bible's view of a person and the one suggested by Professor Joad?

Why might science not be a good tool for testing ideas on life after death?

Do you agree that the idea that we simply rot once we die, takes the value and purpose out of life? Explain your answer.

How is reincarnation explained in *A Sneaking Suspicion*?

What comfort might a belief in reincarnation bring to a person?

Make sense?

Reincarnation is supposed to result in the world moving towards a state of perfection. Do you think this is actually happening? Explain your answer.

Why might reincarnation not be such a hopeful idea after all?

Solve or create evil

Draw a diagram to show the argument that reincarnation creates evil rather than solves it. (pages 90–91)

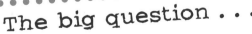

The big question . . .

What do you think will happen to you after you die?

Chapter 11

THE LIFE FACTOR

Whom can you trust?

We die only once and then we are judged. (Hebrews 9:27 CEV)

In what three ways is this message different from the previous two views expressed in chapter 10?

-
-
-

What questions do you have regarding the argument that Jesus is the expert on death? Do you agree?

> It's not that I'm afraid to die, I just don't want to be there when it happens.
> **Woody Allen.**[1]

V I E W 3 1. Be prepared

The one who dies with the most money wins.
(T-shirt slogan)

Where do you turn to get your answers to questions about death?

In this box summarise your ideas on what happens when we die.

My ideas about death!

 Luke 12:16–20
What do you think?

The things that count

Draw some symbols that show the things that are most important to you – the 'things that count' in life.

---

2. The bad news - we are judged

Read pages 99–100.
John 5:28–29

What is the 'bad news'?

_____
_____
_____

What reaction do you have to this news?

_____
_____
_____

How do you score on the issue of selfishness and pride? Tick the box that best describes the score you would give yourself.

☐ Excellent ☐ Very Good ☐ Good

☐ Poor ☐ Abysmal

---

3. The good news

John 5:24

What is the 'good news'?

_____

How do you feel about this 'news'?

_____
_____

What is the best part of this 'good news' about Jesus?

_____
_____

Read 'Just a shadow' pages 100–101.
Summarise in your own words the key point of the story.

_____
_____
_____

BILLION-DOLLAR QUESTION

What does the author regard as the billion-dollar question?

_____
_____

Do you regard the billion-dollar question as important or unimportant? Give your answer and an explanation.

Important?/Unimportant? – Explain

_____
_____
_____

What is the promise of Jesus when it comes to facing death?

_____
_____
_____

Chapter 12

THE CROOK AND THE CHRIST

Naked

In what sense were the criminals (who were crucified on the cross with Jesus) 'naked'?

'Forgiveness is the answer to the child's dream of a miracle by which what is broken is made whole again, what is soiled is made clean again.'

Dag Hammarskjold[1]

Facing the hangman

On page 104, referring to someone about to be hanged, the writer speaks of the fact that impending death 'wonderfully concentrates the mind'.

Imagine a situation where you knew you were going to 'face the hangman'. Tick the boxes that correspond to the way you would be feeling.

☐ 'Gee, I wish I'd made more money.'

☐ 'Well, I've had a good run – never mind.'

☐ 'What will happen to me after I die?'

☐ 'I hope I am looking my best.'

☐ 'To think of all the time I wasted.'

☐ 'I'd love to see my friends just one more time.'

☐ 'I wonder what God thinks of me?'

Briefly explain your choices.

Failure

Read Luke 23:32–43.

Select words from the list below that correspond to each of the three men who were crucified - Jesus, the first criminal (who shouted abuse at Jesus), and the second criminal (who asked Jesus to remember him in his kingdom).

Criminal 1   **Jesus**   **Criminal 2**

forgiveness, hostility, respect, authority, submission, disbelief, compassion, defiance, bitterness, belief, admission, anger, kindness, soul-searching, rage, mercy, humility, compassion

On page 106 of *A Sneaking Suspicion* the author quotes Albert Einstein, who speaks of the 'hateful power of the human heart'. He says this is as evident in the playground or in the pub as on the battlefield.

In the space draw images to represent things you see happening in the world that reflect this hateful aspect of the human heart.

If you disagree with Einstein, then do the same to represent the goodness of humankind.

On page 106 John Dickson says he looked into his heart and saw failures. What do you think he meant?

Paradise

What does Jesus' reply to the second criminal tell you about: Jesus?

His offer of forgiveness?

On page 107 the author writes about Jesus that he 'didn't offer a method or bunch of rules about how to get on God's side'. What did he offer?

Unlike any other

Read pages 108–109. What makes Jesus so unique?

Chapter 13

THE DARK SIDE OF FORGIVENESS

 Why would the world be a mess without justice?

_____

_____

Read pages 111–112.

 ## The dark side

Complete the following sentences from page 112:

Jesus was not a crook, but . . .

_____

He posed no political threat but . . .

_____

He never spoke of a military takeover but . . .

_____

One innocent man died so that . . .

_____

When Jesus died he . . .

_____

He absorbed . . .

_____

He endured judgement so that . . .

_____

He suffered like hell so that . . .

_____

The blow we deserved . . .

_____

JESUS on the hook

What does the author mean by saying that Jesus was placed 'on the hook'? (page 113)

_____

_____

_____

Why does he think that he is 'literally connected to Jesus' death'?

_____

_____

_____

THE COST OF FORGIVENESS

Without forgiveness there really is no future.

(Desmond Tutu)[1]

He who is devoid of the power to forgive, is devoid of the power to love.

(Rev Martin Luther King Jnr)[2]

Read pages 113–114.
What did the forgiven husband discover about his wife's forgiveness?

_____

_____

Amy Beale
How costly would it have been for the Beale family to forgive their daughter's killers?

_____

_____

What indication is there that they were able to do this?

_____

_____

Forgiveness does not change the past, but it does enlarge the future.

(Paul Boese)[3]

God's forgiveness
In the space write words that capture both sides of forgiveness.

Beautiful side	Dark side

Tick the boxes that you most strongly agree with:

- ☐ Forgiving someone is never easy
- ☐ If someone really hurts me I'll never forgive them
- ☐ Because Jesus took my punishment, God will forgive me
- ☐ I am good at forgiving people
- ☐ If I do something bad I expect others to forgive me
- ☐ If I am really sorry, God will forgive me
- ☐ Jesus' death doesn't have anything to do with me

How should the costliness of God's forgiveness affect the way we respond to Jesus?

_____

What three questions does the writer suggest we ask ourselves? What is your answer to these questions?

Question
1. _____

2. _____

3. _____

My Answer
1. _____
2. _____
3. _____

What is the essence of the Christian belief?

_____

_____

_____

Chapter 14

FROM DESPAIR TO FEAR

 How important do you think the story of Jesus' resurrection is to Christianity?

_____

_____

_____

Resurrection - fact or fantasy?

If it didn't happen Jesus is: | **If it did happen Jesus is:**

- _____ | - _____

- _____ | - _____

- _____ | - _____

- _____ | - _____

- _____ | - _____

- _____ | - _____

Read pages 117–118.
How do we know that the women disciples had given up on Jesus?

_____

_____

'They've now put the life of Jesus into the category of a sentimental memory, a story to be cherished, perhaps, but not one you'd base your life on'.

What category do you put Jesus in? Explain your answer.

_____

_____

_____

_____

The stark reality

Read pages 119–120.
Explain why 'alarm' turned to 'fear' for the women at the tomb.

_____

_____

_____

'I feel terribly sympathetic for the followers of Jesus because I hear hope there; not history.'
(John Dominic Crossan)[1]

What is meant by 'the whole story of Christ crashes in on them'?

_____

_____

_____

 Complete the following phrases:

Sentimentality gave way to . . .

_____

Mere remembrance transformed to . . .

_____

Define 'fear' as suggested as the right response to Jesus' resurrection.

_____

Describe your own reaction to the 'news' of Jesus' resurrection:

_____

_____

_____

_____

 The author of *A sneaking suspicion* says that 'Jesus' resurrection calls on all of us to look into the empty tomb (so to speak) and know, with these women, that Jesus is not a lovely memory from the past; he is the risen King of today'. (page 121)

When you look into the empty tomb what do you see?

_____

_____

Complete the following:
The author recommends that those:

| Whose Christian knowledge stopped growing once they left Sunday School . . . |
| With intellectual doubts . . . |
| Who fear a clash of lifestyles . . . |

 What things get in the way of you being able to see Jesus as someone to 'stake your life on'?

Questions I have:

1. _____
2. _____
3. _____
4. _____

Explain why Paul (the writer of 1 Corinthians) would say that if Christ has not risen, Christians are to be pitied more than all men? How important was the resurrection to him?

_____

_____

WHAT DIFFERENCE A RESURRECTION MAKES
Read page 122. Resurrection means that . . .

- _____
- _____
- _____
- _____
- _____

And if Christ has not been raised, your faith is futile; you are still in your sins. Then those also who have fallen asleep in Christ are lost. If only for this life we have hope in Christ, we are to be pitied more than all men.
(1 Corinthians 15:17–19 NIV)

MORE THAN A HUNCH

Life's puzzle

Read pages 123-124.

In chapter 15 the author likens life to a huge jigsaw puzzle. What is your way of making sense of the puzzle of life? Explain your answer below. Try to include the key that for you, provides the answers to life's big questions:

_____

_____

_____

The key to the puzzle

Read pages 124-126.
Write onto the appropriate puzzle pieces the key ideas presented in *A sneaking suspicion*.

©Chris Morgan   www.cxmedia.com

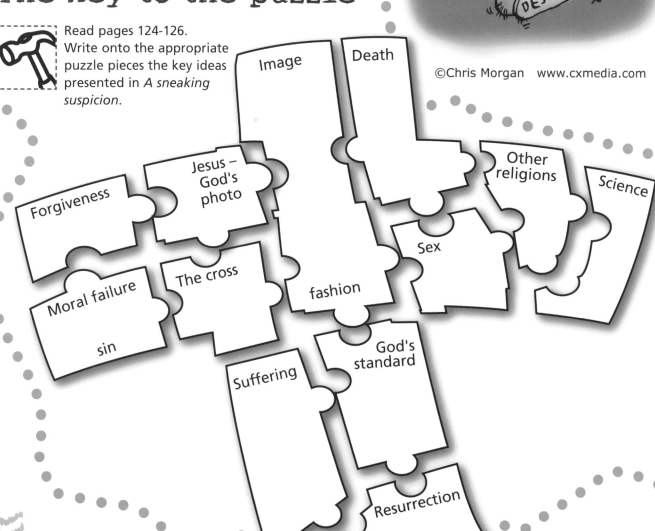

Image

Death

Other religions

Science

Forgiveness

Jesus – God's photo

Sex

Moral failure

The cross

fashion

sin

Suffering

God's standard

Resurrection

The author John Dickson says the longer he is a Christian the more it makes sense to be one. What are his reasons?

Read page 127.
Why did John Dickson write the book?

How successful has he been in his aim? Explain.

How would you describe your reaction to the book?

Interested

sceptical

angry

excited

convinced

questioning

Circle the face that best sums up your reaction to the thoughts presented in the book. Explain your choice:

Sneaking Suspicion
Write down the things about the book you found

positive	negative	interesting

Chapter 16

WHERE TO FROM HERE?

What would you like
to say to God?